the Quiltmaker's Club
More Patterns for Less

10 New Projects From Mary's Cottage Quilts

Colorful Stash Busters

Mary Cowan

C&T PUBLISHING

Text copyright © 2011 by Mary Cowan

Photography copyright © 2011 by C&T Publishing, Inc.

Artwork copyright © 2011 by Mary Cowan

Publisher: Amy Marson

Creative Director: Gailen Runge

Acquisitions Editor: Susanne Woods

Editor: Cynthia Bix

Technical Editors: Teresa Stroin and Gailen Runge

Cover/Book Designer: Kristy Zacharias

Page Layout: Kerry Graham

Production Coordinator: Zinnia Heinzmann

Production Editor: Alice Mace Nakanishi

Illustrator: Tim Manibusan

Photography by Christina Carty-Francis and Diane Pedersen of C&T Publishing, Inc., unless otherwise noted

Published by C&T Publishing, Inc., P.O. Box 1456, Lafayette, CA 94549

Library of Congress Cataloging-in-Publication Data

Cowan, Mary (Mary Stewart)

 Colorful Stash Busters : 10 New Projects from Mary's Cottage Quilts / Mary Cowan.

 pages cm

 ISBN 978-1-60705-271-5 (soft cover)

1. Strip quilting--Patterns. 2. Machine quilting--Patterns. 3. Patchwork--Patterns. I. Title.

 TT835.C697 2011

 746.46--dc22

 2010048108

Printed in China

10 9 8 7 6 5 4 3 2 1

Contents

Dedication

To Scott, Ben, and Melissa,
Thank you for your love and patience;
you guys have always been my biggest fans.
I love you so much!

Acknowledgments

First of all, I want to thank my husband for buying me my first quilting book some 18 years ago. I think he is still kicking himself for that fatal lapse in judgment. I would also like to thank my darling children, who have been more than happy to humor this "queen of reheat" and eat the frozen meals I have put in front of them. Thanks, too, to my cousin Leslie for walking around Wheeler Farms with me and taking my picture for this book.

I especially would like to thank my mom, Regina, and my brother Dan, who have been my cheerleaders from afar; they are always ready with words of encouragement. I would also like to acknowledge my dad, Dudley, whose quiet strength is with me always; he taught me of the beauty in nature that is all around us. Thanks to my family, the Stewarts, whose heritage I am a large part of and whose love I have felt. The name of my company—Mary's Cottage Quilts—is taken from a cottage built by my great-grandfather William James Stewart in upstate New York in 1907. Thanks to all of my family—I love you all!

I know this book wouldn't even be possible without C&T Publishing! How can I ever thank you? You have taken this clueless quilter under your wing, and you have been so nice to work with. You are a team, and I have felt your kindness throughout this whole process. Thank you all for your patience and willingness to help me—Cynthia Bix, Teresa Stroin, Alice Mace Nakanishi, Zinnia Heinzmann, and Kerry Graham.

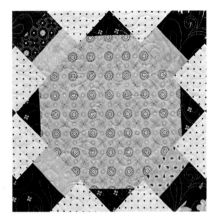

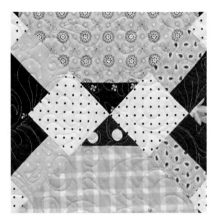

Introduction

When I was in sixth grade, all of my friends decided they hated the color black. I decided that I hated olive green. I look back at that now and laugh, because I actually chose a specific green to hate. I guess I have always been aware of color—how it affects the feel of a quilt or a room, and so on. I remember back to my college days to one of my graphic design professors telling us to look at colors in nature when we are exploring different color combinations.

That being said, I think we quilters sometimes stress way too much about color choices. In this book, my primary goal is to encourage you to let loose a little with your color options.

Last year when I was binding an old quilt for a friend of mine, I noticed that there were a lot of different shades of the same color within the quilt and that they all didn't quite "match." It was like a breath of fresh air to see that this quiltmaker had used what she had on hand—because let's face it, there probably wasn't a local quilt shop nearby with the perfect shade of green. I love that approach! I love to use my stash, see what I can take from it, and then add other fabrics as needed.

For each project in this book, I show you two different color possibilities in the hope that it will help you see that there is always more than one successful colorway for any quilt.

Most of the quilts in this book were based on fabric I had in my stash, with new pieces as needed. Having said that, the guidelines listed for fabric requirements with these quilt projects are the smallest amounts you will want to purchase. Remember, these are guidelines; they are not set in stone. I really want you to use what you have in your stash and then add to it. Sharing fabrics with quilting friends is another great way to build a good variety of fabrics in small amounts!

My second goal in this book is for you to have fun and try new ways to design your quilt tops and put your blocks together. For example, I like to figure out ways to make these quilts a lot easier to construct than they look—often by designing layouts with the blocks on point. I also love to use two different blocks and see the secondary design that is created when these blocks come together. I hope you will take some of the approaches you learn in this book and use them when making other quilts and projects. I also hope this book will be a useful reference tool for you.

But most of all, I want you to have fun with these projects! Make your own color and fabric choices, cut up those fabrics, and have fun sewing them back together to create your own unique and special masterpieces.

—*Mary Cowan*

Sunny Side Up Quilt

Designed and made by Mary Cowan.
Machine quilted by Eagle Mountain Quilting.

FINISHED BLOCK SIZE: 9″ × 9″
FINISHED QUILT SIZE: 65″ × 77⅝″

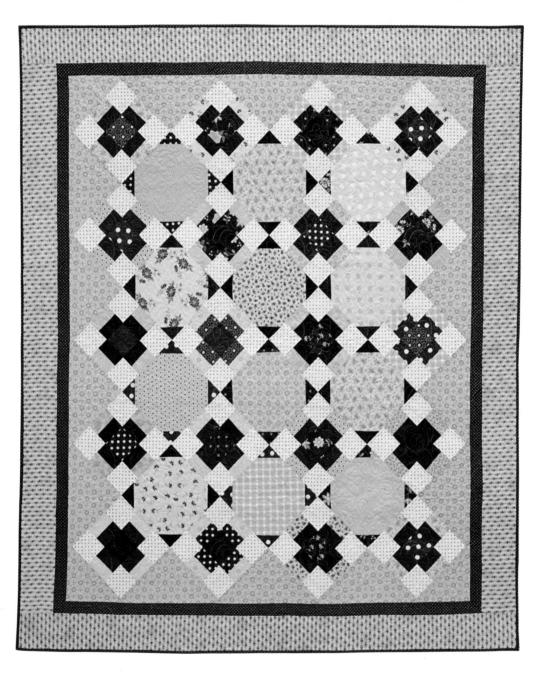

This quilt is the perfect stash buster because it features so many different fabrics. I used red and yellow—my favorite color combination—because these colors look so fresh and happy together. But feel free to choose your own favorites! The on-point layout using two different blocks only looks *complex.*

Materials

Fabric requirements are based on 40"-wide fabric.

- 1⅝ total yards of assorted yellow fabrics for the blocks
- 1⅛ total yards of assorted red fabrics for the blocks
- 1 yard of light fabric for the A's in Block 1
- 1⅜ yards of coordinating yellow fabric for side and corner triangles
- ⅝ yard of red fabric for inner border
- 2 yards of yellow fabric for outer border
- ⅝ yard of red fabric for binding
- 4¼ yards of 54"-wide fabric for backing*
- Twin-size quilt batting

If you prefer, you can use 5 yards of 40"-wide fabric.

Cutting

Instructions are for cutting single blocks; you will need 20 of Block 1 and 12 of Block 2.

BLOCK 1 (FOR *EACH*)

- Cut 4 squares (A) 3½" × 3½" from light fabric.
- Cut 4 rectangles (B) 2" × 3½" from yellow fabrics.
- Cut 4 rectangles (C) 2" × 3½" from red fabrics.
- Cut 1 square (D) 3½" × 3½" from red fabric (use a different red than for C).

BLOCK 2 (FOR *EACH*)

- Cut 1 square (A) 9½" × 9½" from yellow fabric.
- Cut 4 squares (B) 2¾" × 2¾" from red fabrics. (I made my reds the same within a block, but you don't have to.)

SIDE TRIANGLES

- Cut 2 strips 16½" × width of fabric; subcut into 4 squares 16½" × 16½". Cut each square diagonally *twice* to make 16 side triangles. (You need only 14; you will have 2 left over.)

CORNER TRIANGLES

- Cut 1 strip 13" × width of fabric; subcut into 2 squares 13" × 13". Cut each square diagonally *once* to make 4 triangles.

BORDERS

- Cut 7 strips 2½" × width of fabric for inner border.
- Cut 4 strips 5" × *length* of fabric for outer border.

BINDING

- Cut 8 strips 2¼" × width of fabric; sew together using diagonal seams.

For this alternate colorway, I used some Civil War reproduction fabrics to give it a totally different look. I think it looks very vintage.

Making the Blocks

Block 1

The following instructions are for 1 block. You will need a total of 20 blocks.

1. Sew B to C and press toward C. Repeat to make a total of 4.

2. For the top and bottom rows of the block, sew an A to each side of B/C and press toward A. Repeat to make a total of 2.

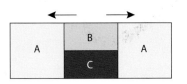

3. For the middle block row, sew a B/C to each side of D as shown and press toward D.

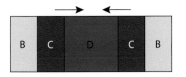

4. Sew the rows together as shown and press toward the top and bottom rows.

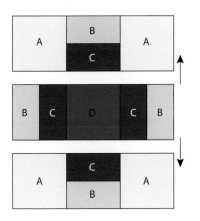

Block 2

The following instructions are for 1 block. You will need a total of 12 blocks.

1. Draw a diagonal line corner to corner on the wrong side of all the B squares.

2. Lay out an A square and place 4 B's on top as shown with right sides together. Pin and sew on the diagonal lines.

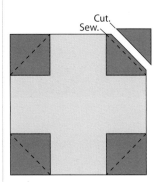

3. Trim off the corners ¼" past the stitching line (as shown above). Fold the B's over and press.

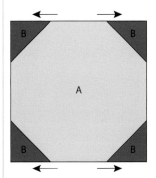

Assembling the Quilt Top

1. Refer to the quilt assembly diagram to lay out the blocks in diagonal rows; be sure to include the side triangles. (You will wait until all the rows are sewn together before you sew on the corners.)

> **Tip**
>
> *The side and corner triangles are cut large, and will stick out on the sides of the quilt—this is okay! You'll trim them later.*

2. Pin and stitch the blocks into rows, then press.

3. Sew together the rows, then sew on the 4 corners. Press.

4. To trim the quilt top, place it on your cutting mat and use a wide plastic ruler and rotary cutter to straighten up the edges and remove the excess fabric. To "float" the middle of this quilt, leave a ¾" seam allowance when trimming. Make sure that opposite sides of the quilt are the same length and that the corners are right angles.

5. This quilt has butted borders. Refer to Quiltmaking Basics (page 57) to measure and sew the inner and outer borders.

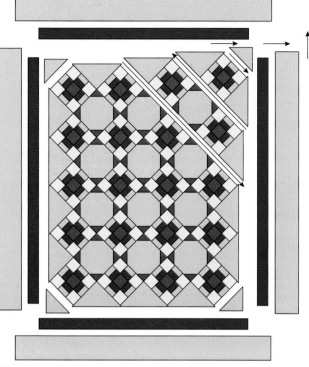

Quilt assembly diagram

Finishing the Quilt

Refer to Quiltmaking Basics (pages 57–60) to layer, quilt, and bind your quilt.

Wild Webs Quilt

Designed and made by Mary Cowan.
Custom machine quilted by Linda Engar.

FINISHED BLOCK SIZE: 15½″ × 15½″
FINISHED QUILT SIZE: 57½″ × 57½″

The traditional way to make Spider Webs is to use paper piecing; instead, I used a special triangle ruler that made it so much easier! I created these Spider Webs totally from my stash of scraps. Just have fun making this—it's very easy, and the outer edges of the webs are ragged for added texture.

Materials

- Scraps of bright-colored fabrics (a good variety is a must!) for webs and sashing posts*

- 4 yards of light fabric for block backgrounds, sashing, and border

- 3¾ yards of fabric for backing

- ½ yard of fabric for binding

- Twin-size quilt batting

- Tri-Recs Tools Tri Tool (triangular ruler; see Resources, page 62)

This quilt can also be made out of a precut strip bundle. The difference will be that you won't have strips that are of varying widths.

Cutting

FABRIC SCRAPS

- Cut strips 2½", 3½", or 4" × longest measurement of fabric.*

- Cut 4 squares 2" × 2" for the sashing posts.

LIGHT FABRIC

Before cutting, reserve a 20" × 60" piece for the borders.

- Cut 9 squares 16" × 16" for the block backgrounds.

- Cut 12 strips 2" × 16" for the sashing.

- Cut 4 strips 4½" × 60" along the *length* of fabric for the borders.

BINDING

- Cut 7 strips 2¼" × width of fabric; sew together using diagonal seams.

* I used scraps, so I cut strips, matched some up, and sewed them together, repeating these steps many times until I had the amount I needed.

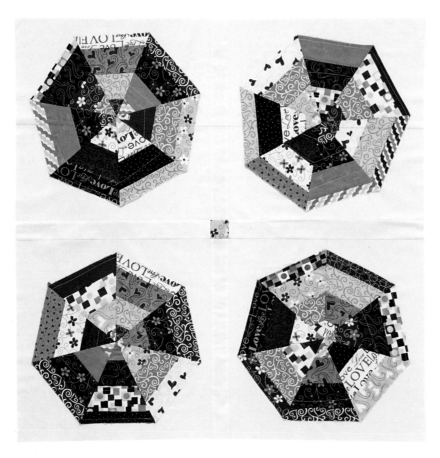

I used a precut strip bundle (40 strips 2½" × 45") for this alternate colorway, so it has a less scrappy look than the original quilt, which I made from my stash fabrics, and the strips are a uniform width instead of varying widths. To vary the width of the top and bottom strips, change the placement of the Tri Tool when trimming to a triangle shape (Step 2, page 15).

Making the Web Blocks

Make 9 blocks.

1. For the webs, sew together 4 strips of different fabrics in varying widths along the long edges to make strip sets. Depending on the width of your strips, you can use more or fewer than 4, but the finished width of the strip set must be at least 7½". Press.

2. Center the Tri Tool top to bottom on your strip set so that you cut out a complete triangle shape. To get the greatest number of triangles out of each strip set, alternately flip the tool as shown. Cut a total of 63 triangles. You need 7 triangles to make each complete web.

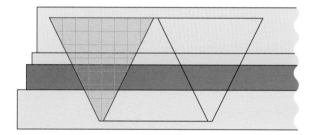

3. Pick 7 triangles that look nice together and sew them together to complete 1 web. Repeat for a total of 9 webs.

4. Cut off the dog ears that hang down past the outer edges of the webs.

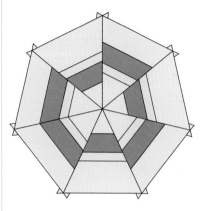

5. Center the completed web on a 16" × 16" background square. Pin very well and sew it to the background, starting in the middle and working out to the edges. Leave the outer edges raw so they will fray when you wash them. I sewed a funky concentric circular pattern just to hold the webs in place; the final quilting did the job of anchoring them firmly. Make sure you sew no closer than ¼" to the outer edge of the web so it will fray nicely.

Assembling the Quilt Top

1. Refer to the quilt assembly diagram to lay out the blocks in 3 rows; place sashing pieces between the blocks only, not at the ends of the rows. Sew together each row.

2. You will need 2 strips of sashing with posts to place between the rows. To make a sashing strip, sew together as follows: sashing piece, post, sashing piece, post, sashing piece, as shown. Repeat for the other sashing.

3. Sew together the rows and sashing. Press toward the sashing.

4. This quilt has butted borders. Please refer to Quiltmaking Basics (page 57) to measure and sew the inner and outer borders.

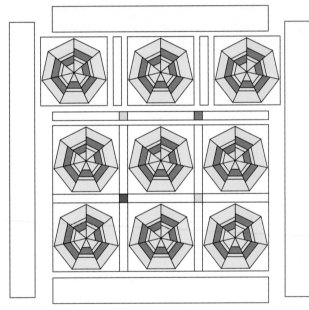

Quilt assembly diagram

Finishing the Quilt

Note: You will need to wash the quilt to rag the webs, but do not wash it until after finishing.

Refer to Quiltmaking Basics (pages 57–60) to layer, quilt, and bind your quilt. I had this quilt custom machine quilted. I love what Linda did here with the flowers and the swirls.

Ragging the Webs

Throw the finished quilt in the washer and wash in *cold* water with 1 cup of distilled white vinegar (to set the colors). Toss it in the dryer; when it is dry, your webs will have the desired "ragged" look. If some of the web edges are not frayed enough, you can squirt them with plain water from a squirt bottle, brush with a soft brush, and put the quilt back in the dryer.

Now your quilt is done!

Mad Hatter Quilt

Designed and made by Mary Cowan.
Custom machine quilted by Linda Engar.

FINISHED BLOCK SIZE: 7¾″ × 7¾″
FINISHED QUILT SIZE: 52¾″ × 68¼″

Cheeseburgers? Easter eggs? Spaceships? I don't really know what these things are, but they sure were fun to make! The block is both pieced and appliquéd; the rickrack adds extra texture. I used a fat quarter bundle, but you really could make it out of scraps from your stash.

Materials

Fabric requirements are based on 40"-wide fabric.

- 23 coordinating fat quarters for A and C block pieces*
- ⅝ yard of fabric for B block pieces
- 8¼ yards of rickrack
- ½ yard of fabric for inner border
- 1¾ yards of fabric for outer border
- 3½ yards of fabric for backing
- ½ yard of fabric for binding
- Twin-size quilt batting
- Spray starch
- 1 sheet of heat-resistant template plastic (see Resources, page 62)

* You could probably get by with about 18 fat quarters, but I used 23 because I liked the variety.

Cutting

BLOCKS

- Cut 66 rectangles 4" × 8½" from the fat quarters (A).
- Cut 33 rectangles 1½" × 8½" (B).

BORDERS

- Cut 5 strips 2½" × width of fabric for inner border.
- Cut 4 strips 5½" × *length* of fabric for outer border.

BINDING

- Cut 7 strips 2¼" × width of fabric. Sew together using diagonal seams.

> **Tip**
>
> *Choose your rickrack first and match your fabrics to it, or you'll end up having to dye your rickrack to match the fabric—an interesting activity I wouldn't recommend!*

> **Tip**
>
> *I didn't cut out all of my A's at once. I constructed about 25 of the 33 blocks needed, laid them out on the floor, and moved them around. I decided which colors and color combinations I needed more of, and then I cut and constructed the remaining blocks.*

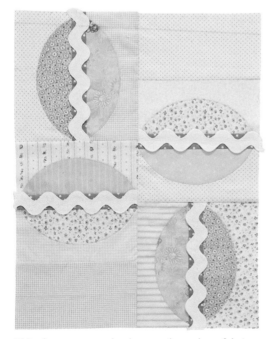

This alternate pastel colorway shows how fabric choices can really affect the look of a quilt design!

Preparing the C Pieces

Use the piece C template pattern (page 21).

1. To make a template for piece C, trace the outline of the template pattern onto the heat-resistant template plastic and cut it out with scissors.

2. On the *wrong* sides of your fat quarter fabrics, position the template and cut out 66 pieces. Important: On the curved side *only*, cut out each piece ¼" larger than the traced line to create a turn-under allowance. I mixed up the fabrics for piece C. I just wanted them to contrast with the background piece (A).

3. Apply spray starch to the wrong side of the curved side of C and place the C template on the wrong side of C. Align the straight edge of the template with the straight edge of the fabric, fold the curved edge over onto the template, and iron it with a dry iron on the cotton setting. This will produce the nicest curve you have ever seen!

Making the Blocks

The following instructions are for 1 block; you will need a total of 33 blocks. All seams are ¼″ unless otherwise specified.

1. Place C on top of A, with the wrong side of C to the right side of A. The straight edge of C should match a long edge of A, and C should be centered on A from top to bottom as shown. Pin.

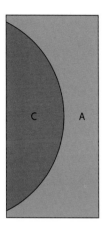

2. Topstitch C to A using a blanket, zigzag, or straight stitch—whichever you prefer. Repeat with another A and C for the other side of the block.

Tip

I matched my thread color to the C fabric, but you could use a contrasting thread for a decorative touch.

---

3. Sew a B piece between the 2 halves of the block and press the seams toward B.

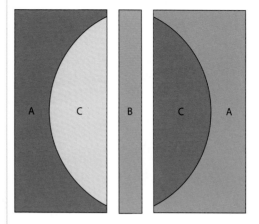

4. Trim the block to 8¼″ × 8¼″.

5. Cut a piece of rickrack 8¼″ long, pin it down the middle of B, and topstitch with matching thread.

6. Repeat Steps 1–5 to make a total of 33 blocks.

Assembling the Quilt Top

1. Refer to the quilt assembly diagram (page 20) to lay out the quilt top. Note that some blocks are oriented vertically and others horizontally to give the design movement. The blocks are laid out in 5 columns. Columns 1, 3, and 5 have 7 blocks each. Columns 2 and 4 have 6 blocks each. You will need an extra half-block on the top and bottom of columns 2 and 4. Choose 4 of your favorite fabrics and cut 4 rectangles 4⅜″ × 8¼″. Add these to columns 2 and 4 and then move all the blocks around until you like the way they look.

2. Sew together the blocks in each column. Press.

3. Sew together the columns. Press.

4. This quilt has butted borders. Refer to Quiltmaking Basics (page 57) to measure and sew the inner and outer borders.

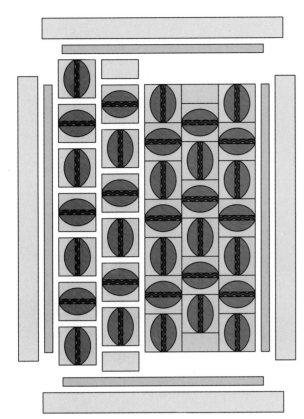

Finishing

Refer to Quiltmaking Basics (pages 57–60) to layer, quilt, and bind your quilt.

Quilt assembly diagram

Piece C

Cut 66.

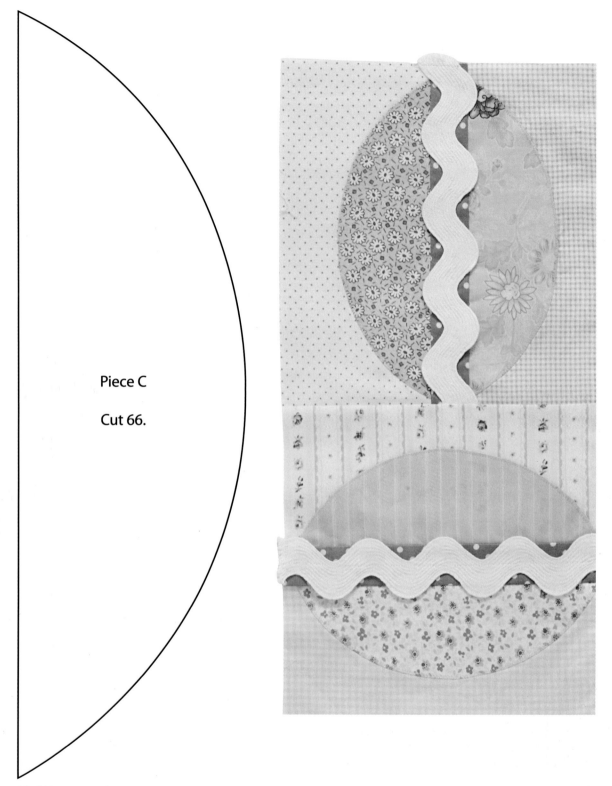

Mad Hatter template pattern

Summer Sky Quilt

Designed and made by Mary Cowan.
Custom machine quilted by Connie Atkisson.

FINISHED BLOCK SIZE: 12″ × 12″
FINISHED QUILT SIZE: 71¼″ × 71¼″

I love the rich, dark look of Civil War reproduction fabric! I have quite a stash of it that I was able to use for most of the blocks in this quilt. In this diagonal set design, the black setting triangles combined with the red inner border make the blocks in the middle just pop.

Materials

Fabric requirements are based on 40"-wide fabric.

- 1¾ yards (total) of assorted light fabrics for block pieces A, B, and D*
- 1½ yards (total) of assorted dark fabrics for block pieces C, E, and F*
- ½ yard of red fabric for inner border
- 1⅜ yards of black fabric for side and corner triangles (This is the same fabric as the sashing, posts, and outer border.)
- 2⅛ yards of black fabric for sashing, posts, and outer border (This is the same fabric as the side and corner triangles. Cut the 2 pieces separately so as to have enough fabric to cut the outer border strips on the lengthwise grain.)
- 4½ yards of fabric for backing
- ⅝ yard of fabric for binding
- Full-size quilt batting

* I used a lot of scraps from my stash, plus fat quarters for variety.

> **Tip**
>
> *I wanted this quilt to have a very scrappy look, so I tried to make all of the lights and darks within one block out of different fabrics. I did keep the frames the same color within each block.*

Cutting

BLOCKS

From the assorted lights:

- Cut 52 squares 2½" × 2½" (A).
- Cut 52 squares 3⅞" × 3⅞" (B).
- Cut 52 squares 3½" × 3½" (D).

From the assorted darks:

- Cut 52 squares 3⅞" × 3⅞" (C).
- Cut 26 rectangles 1½" × 4½" (E).
- Cut 26 rectangles 1½" × 6½" (F).

SIDE TRIANGLES

- From the 1⅜ yards of black fabric, cut 2 strips 22" × width of fabric; subcut into 2 squares 22" × 22". Cut these diagonally *twice* to make 8 side triangles.

CORNER TRIANGLES

- From the leftover side triangle strips, cut 2 squares 13" × 13". Cut these diagonally *once* to make 4 corner triangles.

BORDERS

- From the red fabric, cut 6 strips 2½" × width of fabric for inner border.
- From the 2⅛ yards of black fabric, cut 4 strips 6" × *length* of fabric for outer border.

> **Tip**
>
> *Cut the long borders 6" × length of fabric first; then cut the sashing pieces and posts out of the leftover border fabric.*

SASHING AND POSTS

- From the leftover border fabric, cut 7 strips 1¼" × *length* of fabric.

  Subcut into 36 rectangles 1¼" × 12½" for the sashing.

  Subcut into 24 squares 1¼" × 1¼" for the posts.

> **Tip**
>
> *For this project, I chose to make the posts the same color as the sashing. I prefer to have posts with sashing, as they give you a reference point as to where your blocks should line up with each other to make your rows straight. To me it is so much harder to align the rows when there is just sashing and no posts.*

BINDING

- Cut 8 strips 2¼" × width of fabric; sew together using diagonal seams.

For the alternate colorway, I chose red and cream with bold dark frames around the four-patches. I think it gives this block a very different look. To add corner posts in an alternate color, as I did, use scraps that you have on hand or buy an extra ⅛ yard of a light fabric, cut 1 strip 1¼" × width of fabric, and subcut into 24 squares 1¼" × 1¼".

Making the Blocks

Each block has a framed four-patch unit in the center, surrounded by 8 half-square triangle (HST) units and 4 solid units.

Half-Square Triangles

You will need a total of 104 HSTs for all the blocks. You will be able to get 2 out of each pair of B and C squares.

> ### Tip
> *I constructed these all at once and put them together randomly—I just picked a B and a C, pinned them together, and sewed them without agonizing over the selections.*

1. Draw a diagonal line corner to corner on the wrong side all of the B squares.

2. Place a B square on top of a C square with right sides together. Sew a *scant* ¼" seam on each side of the drawn diagonal line as shown. Cut apart on the drawn line, press, and square up to 3½" × 3½". Repeat with all of the B's and C's to complete 104 HSTs. Set these aside for now.

Sew first.

Cut last.

Four-Patches

The following instructions are for 1 four-patch unit for 1 block; you will need to make 13 of these units.

1. Select and sew together 4 A's. Press.

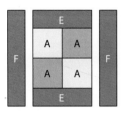

2. To frame the four-patch, sew an E strip to the top and bottom of the four-patch. Press toward the E's. Sew an F strip to each side and press toward the F's.

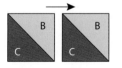

Block Assembly

The following instructions are for 1 block; you will need to make a total of 13 blocks.

1. Sew together 2 of the HSTs for the top row of the block, placing the dark halves as shown. Press toward the C.

2. Sew a D square to each end of the HST unit. Press toward the D's.

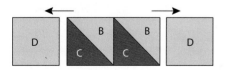

3. Repeat Steps 1 and 2 for the bottom row of the block, placing the dark HSTs in the same position as in Step 1.

4. Sew together 2 sets of the HSTs for the sides of the block. Press toward the C. *Note:* The darks are placed differently than for the top and bottom rows. Study the block assembly diagram carefully!

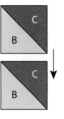

5. Referring to the block assembly diagram, sew the HST side units to the side of the framed four-patch. Press toward the framed four-patch.

6. Sew the top and bottom rows to the framed four-patch. Press toward the framed four-patch.

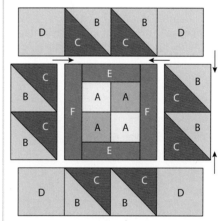

Block assembly diagram

Assembling the Quilt Top

1. Refer to the quilt assembly diagram to lay out the blocks in 5 diagonal rows; be sure to include the side triangles. (You will wait until all the rows are sewn together before you sew on the corners.)

2. Place sashing between blocks in a row and at the ends of each row between the blocks and the triangles.

3. Pin and sew the blocks, sashing, and side triangles into rows. Press toward the sashing.

4. Sew together the sashing for the vertical rows. You will need 2 rows with 1 sashing piece and 2 posts (on the outer ends), 2 rows with 3 pieces of sashing and 4 posts, and 2 rows with 5 pieces of sashing and 6 posts. Press toward the sashing.

5. To complete the top, pin and sew together the rows, including side triangles, with sashing placed between the rows. Press in one direction. Add the corner triangles and press toward the sashing.

6. To trim the quilt top, place it on your cutting mat and use a wide plastic ruler and rotary cutter to straighten up the edges and remove the excess fabric. To "float" the middle of this quilt, leave a ¾″ seam allowance when trimming. Make sure that opposite sides of the quilt are the same length and that the corners are right angles.

7. This quilt has butted borders. Please refer to Quiltmaking Basics (page 57) to measure and sew the inner and outer borders.

Quilt assembly diagram

Finishing

Refer to Quiltmaking Basics (pages 57–60) to layer, quilt, and bind your quilt.

Fun House Baby Quilt

Designed and made by Mary Cowan.
Custom machine quilted by Linda Engar.

FINISHED QUILT SIZE: 42½″ × 43½″

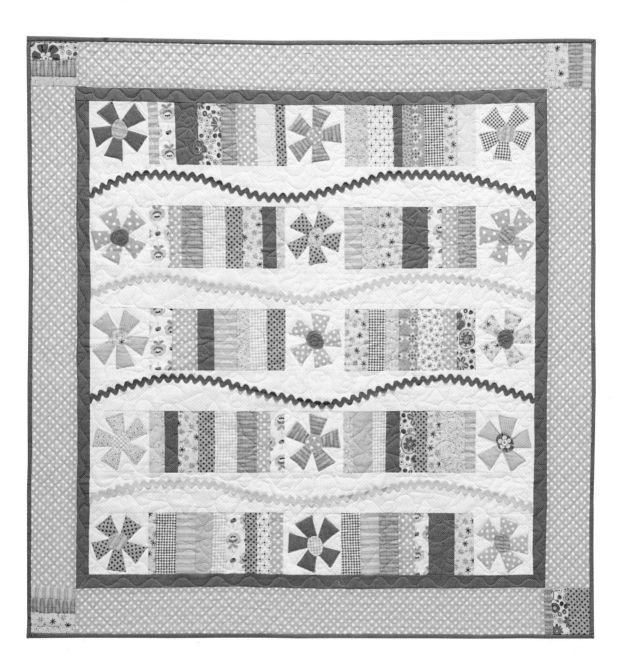

I think pink and green look so cute and girly. I thought this quilt had to have appliquéd flowers in it, too. I used a lot of pinks and limey greens from my stash and bought just a few to add to them. A little boy's version (page 29) features primary colors and turtles instead of flowers! (I offer appliqué patterns for both.) Rickrack adds the finishing touch in both quilts.

Materials

Fabric requirements are based on 40"-wide fabric.

- 1¼ yards total of assorted pink fabrics for strip blocks, appliqué flowers, and border posts (I used scraps from my stash.)

- 1¼ yards total of assorted green fabrics for strip blocks, appliqué flowers, and border posts (I used scraps from my stash.)

- 1 yard of light fabric for appliqué backgrounds and for sashing

- ⅝ yard of bright pink fabric for inner border and binding

- ⅝ yard of green dot fabric for outer border

- 1½ yards of 54"-wide fabric for backing*

- 2 yards of bright pink ⅝"-wide rickrack

- 2 yards of bright green ⅝"-wide rickrack

- Throw-size quilt batting

- Thread to match flower petals, flower centers, and rickrack

- 2 sheets of Quilter's Freezer Paper, 8½" × 11" (see Resources, page 62)

- Spray starch

- Small paintbrush

* If you prefer, you can use 2 yards of 40"-wide fabric and piece the back.

Cutting

STRIP BLOCKS

- Cut 10–15 strips* of assorted pink and green fabrics or scraps in various widths ranging from 1¼" to 2½" × longest measurement of the fabric.

APPLIQUÉ BLOCK BACKGROUNDS

- Cut 2 strips 5" × width of fabric; subcut into 15 squares 5" × 5".

SASHING

- Cut 4 strips 3½" × width of fabric; subcut each strip to 3½" × 34".

BORDERS

- Cut 4 strips 1½" × width of fabric for inner border.

- Cut 4 strips 4" × width of fabric for outer border.

BINDING

- Cut 5 strips 2¼" × width of fabric; sew together using diagonal seams.

* The number of strips will vary depending on sizes of fabric used. See the Tip on page 29.

Tip

Choose your rickrack first and match your fabrics to it, or you'll end up having to dye your rickrack to match the fabric—an interesting activity I wouldn't recommend!

A cute boy's version of this quilt is fun to make in primary colors, with different polka dot fabrics and appliquéd turtles instead of flowers!

Making the Blocks

This quilt has a total of 10 strip blocks and 15 appliqué blocks. All seams are ¼″ unless otherwise specified.

> ## Tip
> *I cut strips from my stash scraps, matched some up, and sewed them together. I repeated these steps many times until I had the amount I needed. (I used seven to eight strips per set.)*

Strip Blocks

1. Sew the pink and green strips together, press, and trim to 5″ × 10½″. You will need a total of 10 sets. Set aside.

2. Out of the remaining pink and green strips, sew a few together and cut into 4 squares 4″ × 4″. These are the posts for the corners of the outer border. Set aside.

Appliqué Blocks

Use the flower template patterns below.

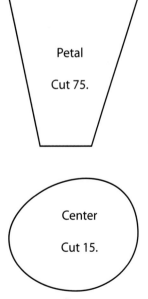

Petal

Cut 75.

Center

Cut 15.

Fun House flower patterns

You will need 5 petals and 1 center per flower for a total of 75 petals and 15 flower centers. I reversed the petal and center colors; if I chose pink for the petals, then I used green for the center, and vice versa. I used the following freezer paper appliqué method, but you can use any method you are comfortable with. I am very appliqué challenged, and I have found that this method works the best for me—except for a couple of burned fingers, that is!

1. Trace each appliqué pattern onto the dull side of a piece of freezer paper. Place each traced pattern on top of 2 additional pieces of freezer paper, all with the dull side facing up. Iron the 3 layers together. This makes very sturdy templates you can use over again. Cut out the 3-layered templates on the solid lines.

> ## Tip
>
> I found I could reuse each template about 5 times. You need a total of 75 petals, so you will cut about 15 of these templates. You can get away with fewer templates (about 3) for the 15 centers.

2. To make a petal, place the template shiny side down on the *wrong* side of your fabric. Iron it in place, using a hot, dry iron.

3. Cut out around the pattern, adding a *scant ¼"* turn-under allowance around all the edges. Leave the template on the fabric.

4. Spray some starch into a cup or the top of the can. With the template still on the fabric, use a small paintbrush to "paint" the fabric seam allowances with starch.

(The flower center will overlap the inner ends of the petals, so you do not need to turn those under.)

5. Press the wet seam allowance over the template pattern using a hot, dry iron. Let the piece cool; then take out the paper template and reuse it to make more petals and centers.

6. Repeat Steps 1–5 to make a total of 75 petals and 15 centers.

7. For each block, arrange 5 petals around 1 center on the background square. The center should overlap the inner ends of the petals. Pin in place.

8. Using a tiny zigzag stitch and thread to match the petals and centers, stitch around the edges of the fabric petals and centers to secure them to the background square.

Assembling the Quilt Top

1. Refer to the quilt assembly diagram (page 31) to lay out 5 rows of 3 appliqué blocks and 2 strip blocks each. Sew together the blocks and press.

2. Sew together the rows and sashing. Press the seams toward the sashing.

3. Arrange a length of pink or green rickrack in a nice, gentle curvy line on top of each sashing strip as shown; pin. Topstitch in place using matching thread. Trim even with the ends of the rows.

Borders

Refer to Quiltmaking Basics (page 57) to measure, cut, and sew on the inner borders. The outer border is a little different because of the corner posts, so follow the special instructions given here.

1. Measure the width of the top and bottom of the quilt and write down that measurement.

2. Measure the length of the sides of the quilt. Cut 2 of your outer border strips to this measurement and sew them to the sides of your quilt. Press toward the border.

3. Cut the remaining 2 outer border strips to the measurement from Step 1. Sew your previously cut 4″ × 4″ corner posts to the ends of these border strips and press toward the border. Sew the borders to the top and bottom of the quilt. Make sure the corners of the posts line up with the corners of the inner border! Press toward the borders.

Quilt assembly diagram

Finishing

Refer to Quiltmaking Basics (pages 57–60) to layer, quilt, and bind—and enjoy this darling baby quilt!

Turtle Appliqués

Use the turtle template patterns below.

I made the turtles using the fusible raw-edge appliqué method because the small pieces would have been tricky to turn under. For this, you will need 1 yard of double-sided fusible web, such as Heat*n*Bond Lite (see Resources, page 62). For the 15 turtles, I used scraps of a solid green fabric for the head and legs and a variety of polka dot fabrics for the shells. I stitched them on with thread to match.

For each turtle, make 1 head, 1 shell, and 2 legs.

1. Trace the templates onto the dull side of the fusible web and cut them out about ¼" outside the traced lines. Follow the manufacturer's instructions to fuse them to the fabrics. *Note:* I reversed some of the heads so my turtles would be facing both ways. To prevent the shells from being too stiff, I cut out the center of the web shape before fusing it, leaving just enough to adhere the shell to the fabric.

2. Cut out the fused pieces and position the pieces for 1 turtle on each background square. At this point, iron on *only* the legs and head. Stitch them down using a tiny zigzag stitch. Then position the shell to very slightly overlap the head and legs, fuse, and stitch.

3. If you wish, use 2 strands of embroidery floss to add a couple of French knots for eyes and to backstitch a mouth.

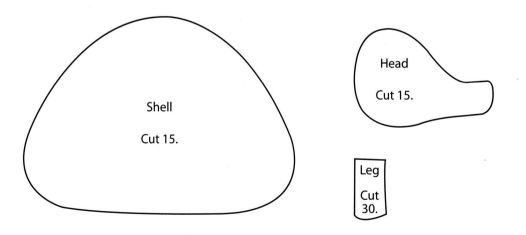

Fun House turtle patterns

King's Cross Station Quilt

Designed by Mary Cowan and made by Valerie Marsh.
Custom machine quilted by Eagle Mountain Quilting.

FINISHED BLOCK SIZE: 10½″ × 10½″
FINISHED QUILT SIZE: 58½″ × 73⅜″

This quilt started with a turquoise print fabric. I fell so in love with it that I bought eight yards! I think the turquoise and the assorted dark chocolates, creams, and brick reds from my stash look so nice together. The pattern created by the on-point setting, plus the dark setting triangles, looks so dramatic. Stash fabrics work really well here because you only need small pieces of the different colors.

Materials

Fabric requirements are based on 40"-wide fabric.

- ⅔ yard total of assorted red fabrics for the blocks

- 1¾ yards total of assorted turquoise fabrics for the blocks

- ⅝ yard total of assorted cream fabrics

- ½ yard total of assorted brown fabrics

- 1⅝ yards of brown fabric for side and corner triangles

- ½ yard of red fabric for inner border

- 2 yards of turquoise fabric for outer border

- 3⅞ yards of fabric for backing

- ⅝ yard red fabric for binding

- Twin-size quilt batting

Tip

It's a good idea to have plenty of stash fabrics so you can select a good variety of light and dark values in the turquoise fabrics, as well as a wide selection of reds—the more variety the better. My friend Valerie made this quilt, and after I dropped off all of the fabric at her house, I thought my stash bags would be lighter—but they still feel just as full! What's up with that? How does that happen?

Cutting

BLOCKS

Assorted reds:

- Cut 108 squares 2" × 2" (A).

- Cut 18 squares 2½" × 2½" (H).

Assorted turquoises:

- Cut 72 rectangles 2" × 8" (B).

- Cut 72 rectangles 2" × 5" (C).

Assorted creams:

- Cut 72 squares 2" × 2" (D).

- Cut 18 squares 2½" × 2½" (G).

Assorted browns:

- Cut 36 squares 2" × 2" (E).

- Cut 18 rectangles 2" × 5" (F).

SIDE TRIANGLES

- Cut 2 strips 18½" × width of fabric; subcut into 3 squares 18½" × 18½". Cut these squares diagonally *twice* to make 12 side triangles. (You will have 2 extra.)

CORNER TRIANGLES

- Cut 1 strip 14" × width of fabric; subcut into 2 squares 14" × 14". Cut these diagonally *once* to make 4 corner triangles.

BORDERS

- Cut 6 strips 2" × width of fabric for inner border.

- Cut 4 strips 5½" × *length* of fabric for outer border.

BINDING

- Cut 8 strips 2¼" × width of fabric; sew together using diagonal seams.

Here's a bright and cheery alternate colorway featuring my favorite color combination—red and yellow.

Making the Blocks

All seams are ¼″ unless otherwise specified.

Each block has a center with a cross design surrounded by a double border. The following instructions make 1 block. You will need a total of 18 blocks.

1. For the block center, sew a D square to each side of an E square. Press toward E. Repeat for the other side of the center.

2. Sew an F piece between the 2 D/E pieces and press toward F. Your block center should now measure 5″ × 5″.

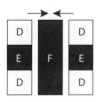

3. For the first block border, sew 2 C pieces to each side of the block center. Press toward the C's.

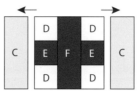

4. Sew an A piece to each short side of a C piece. Press toward C. Repeat to make a second A/C/A piece.

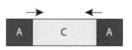

5. Sew the A/C/A pieces to the top and bottom of the block center to complete the first block border. Press toward the border. This should now measure 8″ × 8″.

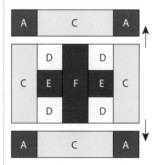

6. For the outer block border, sew a B to each side of the block. Press toward the B's.

7. To make 2 half-square triangles (HSTs), draw a diagonal line corner to corner on the wrong side of the G pieces. Place a G piece on top of an H piece with right sides together and sew a *scant* ¼″ on each side of the drawn diagonal line. Cut apart on the drawn line and press toward the H's. Trim and square up to 2″ × 2″. You will be trimming approximately 1/16″–1/8″, so make sure you split your trimming evenly between all the sides.

Sew first.
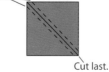
Cut last.

8. For the top border, sew 1 HST to the right end of B, with the red half positioned as shown in the block assembly diagram. Sew an A to the left end of B and press both seams toward the B strip. Sew to the top of the block.

9. For the bottom border, sew 1 HST to the left end of B as shown and an A to the right end. Press both seams toward B. Sew to the bottom of the block. The block should now measure 11″ × 11″.

10. Repeat Steps 1–9 to make 18 blocks.

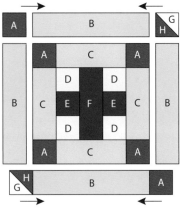

Block assembly diagram

Assembling the Quilt Top

1. Refer to the quilt assembly diagram to lay out the blocks in 6 diagonal rows; be sure to include the side triangles. (You will wait until all the rows are sewn together before you sew on the corners.)

> **Tip**
>
> *The side and corner triangles are cut larger and will stick out on the sides of the quilt—this is okay! You'll trim them later.*

2. Pin and stitch the blocks into rows and press.

3. Sew together the rows; then sew on the 4 corners. Press.

4. To trim the quilt top, place it on your cutting mat and use a wide plastic ruler and rotary cutter to straighten up the edges and remove the excess fabric. To "float" the middle of this quilt, leave a ¾″ seam allowance when trimming. Make sure that opposite sides of the quilt are the same length and that the corners are right angles.

5. This quilt has butted borders. Please refer to Quiltmaking Basics (page 57) to measure and sew the inner and outer borders.

Quilt assembly diagram

Finishing the Quilt

Refer to Quiltmaking Basics (pages 57–60) to layer, quilt, and bind your quilt.

Jazz It Up Table Runner

Designed and made by Mary Cowan.
Custom machine quilted by Connie Atkisson.

FINISHED TABLE RUNNER SIZE: 21½″ × 50½″

I love ruffles! Along with the wool flower appliqués, I think they add great texture to this table runner. Another cool thing about this project is that you can make it any length or width you want to simply by adding more strips and flowers. You could make it entirely from your stash fabrics because the amounts needed are pretty small.

Materials

Fabric requirements are based on 40"-wide fabric.

- ⅛ yard *each* of 4 or 5 different pink fabrics for pieced strips

- ⅛ yard *each* of 4 or 5 different green fabrics for pieced strips

- ⅛ yard *each* of 4 or 5 different brown fabrics for pieced strips

- 1⅝ yards of light print for appliqué background strips and backing

- ½ yard of light brown fabric for borders (on short ends only)

- ½ yard of brown floral print for ruffle

- 2⅝ yards of light green 1½"-wide rickrack

- ⅓ yard of fabric for binding

- Scraps of wool or wool felt for flowers

- Embroidery floss to match wool scraps

- Thread to match rickrack

- Crib-size quilt batting

- 2 sheets of Quilter's Freezer Paper, 8½" × 11" (see Resources, page 62)

- Fabric glue (*optional*)

- Machine ruffler foot (*optional*)

Tip

A word of advice: Choose your rickrack first, and then you can fall in love with fabric that matches the rickrack—not the other way around. Otherwise, you might end up having to dye rickrack to match your fabric. Been there, done that.

Cutting

PIECED STRIPS

- Cut 4" strips from assorted pinks, greens, and browns; cross-cut into random widths from 1½" to 2½".

APPLIQUÉ BACKGROUND STRIPS

- Cut 2 strips 6" × *length* of fabric (set aside remaining piece for the backing); trim strips to 45".

END BORDERS

- Cut 2 strips 5" × width of fabric.

RUFFLE

- Cut 2 strips 5½" × width of fabric; trim strips down to 40".

BINDING

- Cut 4 strips 2¼" × width of fabric; sew together using diagonal seams. (I used a striped fabric for the binding, so I cut it on the bias.)

I made this red, green, and blue alternate version entirely from my stash scraps. I love the way it turned out—for some reason, it has a summer/patriotic feel about it.

Making the Rows

All seams are ¼" unless otherwise specified.

> **Tip**
>
> *For the strip-pieced rows, I kept colors in the same family together in a row—one row of pinks, one row of greens, and one row of browns. You do not have to do it this way—I encourage you to make this table runner your own!*

1. To make the strip-pieced rows, sew your strips together into 3 long rows that measure approximately 4" × 45" each.

2. Press all the seams in each row in the same direction, trim the rows to 42", and set aside.

3. On each of the 2 appliqué background strips, place a length of rickrack in gentle curves as shown in the photo on page 38.

4. Topstitch both edges of the rickrack using matching thread. You are now ready to appliqué the flowers.

Making the Flower Appliqués

Use the table runner template patterns below.

Make 6 wool flowers. Each flower has a large center and a smaller center, so you will need a total of 6 flowers, 6 large centers, and 6 small centers. I used a freezer paper appliqué method for these, but you can use whatever method you are most comfortable with. Since the fabric is wool, I left the edges raw instead of turning them under.

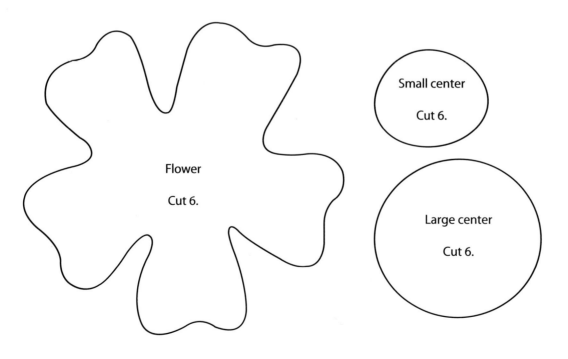

Flower

Cut 6.

Small center

Cut 6.

Large center

Cut 6.

Jazz It Up table runner patterns

1. Trace each appliqué template pattern 6 times onto the dull side of a piece of freezer paper and rough cut the traced patterns.

2. Position the templates on the wool with the shiny side down. Iron in place using the wool setting. The pieces will adhere but won't be permanent.

3. Cut out on the drawn line using sharp scissors; peel off the paper.

4. Position the flowers and centers on top of the rickrack (see the assembly diagram, page 42, for placement). Pin or glue them to your background.

Tip

You will trim the appliqué strips to 42" once everything is appliquéd in place, so don't put your flowers too close to the ends of the rows.

---

5. Now it's time to stitch everything down. I hand stitched the flowers using embroidery floss. The number of strands I use depends on the look I am after. I used 3 strands and a blanket stitch on the petals and large centers, and a whipstitch on the smaller centers. Use whatever stitches you like; for example, you could just do a small running stitch close to the edges of the pieces.

6. When the appliqués are finished, trim the strips to 42" long.

Making the Table Runner Top

To lay out the runner, refer to the assembly diagram (page 42). Sew together the pieced strip rows and appliqué rows and press the seams toward the appliqué rows.

Ruffles

1. To make the ruffles, first finish the short ends of the cut strips. Fold each end under ¼", press, fold under another ¼", and topstitch.

2. Fold each ruffle strip in half with wrong sides together and long edges even. Press.

3. If you have one of those nifty ruffler feet for your sewing machine, follow the manufacturer's instructions to gather the strips. I didn't have one, so I gathered my ruffle the old-fashioned way by running 2 basting stitches ⅛" apart along the unfinished edge of the entire length of the strips and *carefully* pulling the threads to gather the strips.

4. Measure the width of your table runner at each end and gather each ruffle to ½" *shorter* than that measurement. This way, the ruffle won't get stitched down when you bind the edges of the table runner.

5. With the raw edges of the ruffles aligned with the raw edges of the table runner, center and pin each ruffle in place on the right side of the runner, arranging the gathers evenly. Sew on using a long basting stitch. If you are satisfied with the way they look, sew over the basting with a regular length stitch.

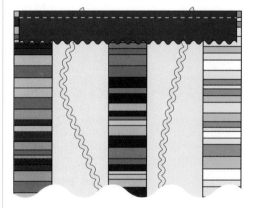

Borders

1. Measure the width of the table runner on the short ends, and cut your 5″ strips to that length.

2. Lay the table runner right side up with the ruffle facing in toward the center of the table runner. Place the border strip right side down on top of the ruffle, with all edges even. Pin and sew. Press toward the border.

Assembly diagram

Finishing

Refer to Quiltmaking Basics (pages 57–60) to layer, quilt, and bind the table runner.

On this runner, in-the-ditch quilting between the ruffle and the body of the table runner helps the ruffle stay put and facing away from the center. The rickrack and flowers are left unquilted.

Tip

When you are sewing the binding, be sure to pin the ruffle out of the way so it doesn't get caught and sewn in the binding by accident.

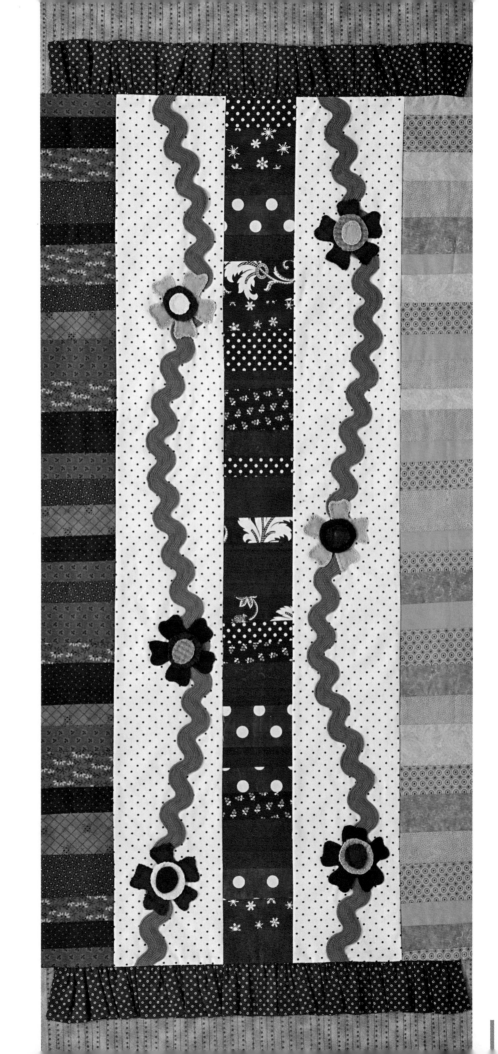

House of Cards Quilt

Designed and made by Mary Cowan.
Custom machine quilted by Holly Williams-Sosa.

FINISHED BLOCK SIZE: 10″ × 10″
FINISHED QUILT SIZE: 79″ × 79″

I love what happens when you put four blocks together and they create a secondary pattern. That's what happened here: I laid the blocks out on the floor and started playing around and moving them, and then I saw the diamond pattern that is created when four lights touch. I used mostly Civil War "shirtings," which are very light.

Materials

Fabric requirements are based on 40"-wide fabric.

- 12–15 fat quarters of assorted light fabrics (I used mostly creams with about 4 or 5 lighter blues thrown in) for block pieces B and C

- ¾ yard total of assorted red fabrics for A's

- 2 yards total of assorted blue fabrics for A's and B's

- 1⅝ yards of dark red fabric for sashing and inner border

- 2⅜ yards of blue fabric for outer border

- 5¼ yards of fabric for backing

- ⅝ yard of fabric for binding

- Full-size batting

> ## Tip
> *Be sure to get a nice variety of reds and blues so that your quilt will sparkle.*

Cutting

BLOCKS

- From the red fabrics, cut 72 squares 2⅞" × 2⅞" (A).

- From the lighter blue fabrics, cut 72 squares 2⅞" × 2⅞" (A).

- From the blue fabrics, cut 18 squares 7" × 7" (B).

- From the light blue and cream fabrics, cut 18 squares 7" × 7" (B).

- From the cream fabrics, cut 144 rectangles 2½" × 6½" (C).

SASHING

- From the dark red fabric, cut 3 strips 10½" × width of fabric; subcut these into 60 rectangles 1½" × 10½".

POSTS

- From the dark blue fabrics, cut 25 squares 1½" × 1½".

BORDERS

- Cut 7 strips 2" × width of fabric for inner border.

- Cut 4 strips 6" × *length* of fabric for outer border.

BINDING

- Cut 9 strips 2¼" × width of fabric; sew together using diagonal seams.

> ## Tip
> - *You can get two complete half-square triangles out of one red A and one blue A.*
>
> - *You can get two complete half-square triangles out of one cream B and one blue B.*

Replacing the cool blues and soft creams with warm yellow and crisp black gives this block an entirely different look!

Making the Blocks

All seams are ¼" unless otherwise specified.

Each block has a large half-square triangle (HST) in the center; some are dark blue and cream, and some are dark blue and light blue. In each corner are small red and blue HSTs.

Half-Square Triangles

You will need a total of 36 large HSTs (1 for each block) and 144 small HSTs (4 for each block). You will be able to get 2 HSTs out of each pair of squares.

1. For the large center HSTs, draw a diagonal line corner to corner on the wrong side of all of the light blue and the cream B squares.

2. Place 1 light B square (either cream or light blue) on top of 1 blue B square with right sides together. Sew a *scant ¼"* seam on each side of the drawn diagonal line. Cut on the drawn line and press toward the darker fabric. Square up to 6½" × 6½". Repeat to make 36 HSTs.

3. For the small corner HSTs, draw a diagonal line corner to corner on the wrong side of all of the red A squares.

4. Place 1 red A square on top of 1 blue A square with right sides together. Sew a *scant ¼"* seam on each side of the drawn diagonal line. Cut on the drawn line and press toward the darker fabric. Square up to 2½" × 2½". Repeat to make 144 HSTs. *Note:* Make the 4 corner pieces from 2 identical pairs if you want to use all the same red and blue within a block like I did.

Block Assembly

The following instructions make 1 block. You will need a total of 36 blocks.

1. Sew a C piece to each side of a large HST. Press.

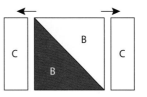

2. With the red and blue positioned as shown, sew a small HST to each end of a C piece. Press toward C. Repeat to make a total of 2.

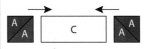

3. Sew the pieces from Step 2 to the top and bottom of the center unit, referring to the block assembly diagram for the correct orientation of the red and blue HSTs in the corners. Press away from the center.

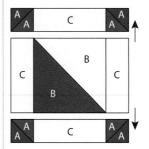

Block assembly diagram

Assembling the Quilt Top

1. Refer to the quilt assembly diagram to lay out 6 rows of 6 blocks each. Place sashing between the blocks but not at the ends of the rows. Sew together the blocks and sashing into rows and press toward the sashing.

2. Make 5 rows with 6 sashing rectangles alternated with 5 posts. Press toward the sashing.

3. Place sashing and post rows between the block rows and sew together. Press toward the sashing.

4. This quilt has butted borders. Refer to Quiltmaking Basics (page 57) to measure and sew the inner and outer borders.

Quilt assembly diagram

Finishing

Refer to Quiltmaking Basics (pages 57–60) to layer, quilt, and bind your quilt.

Endless Possibilities Table Topper

Designed and made by Mary Cowan.
Machine quilted by Eagle Mountain Quilting.

FINISHED BLOCK SIZE: 8″ × 8″
FINISHED QUILT SIZE: 42½″ × 42½″

This is an awesome table topper to whip up using strips or precuts and some yardage. Squares in a diagonal setting make this star design super-easy to achieve. It goes together very quickly and can be used as either a table topper or a baby quilt. The possibilities are endless!

Materials

Fabric requirements are based on 40"-wide fabric.

- 9 strips 1½" × 40" of assorted coordinating fabrics
- ⅓ yard of dark print fabric for star blocks
- ⅝ yard of light print fabric for star and background blocks
- ⅓ yard of medium print fabric for inner border
- 1⅓ yards of dark print fabric for outer border
- 1½ yards of 54"-wide fabric for backing*
- ⅜ yard of fabric for binding
- Crib-size batting

If you prefer, you can use 3 yards of 40"-wide fabric and piece the back.

> ## Tip
> *An easy way to get started is with a Moda Honey Bun. It contains 40 precut strips 1½" × 45" of coordinating fabrics. One Honey Bun is enough to make 4 complete striped stars. Great for gifts!*

Cutting

BLOCKS

- Cut 4 squares 8⅞" × 8⅞" from the dark fabric.
- Cut 4 squares 8⅞" × 8⅞" from the light fabric.

BACKGROUND

- Cut 4 squares 8½" × 8½" from the same light fabric as above.

BORDERS

- Cut 4 strips 2" × width of fabric for inner border.
- Cut 4 strips 4¼" × *length* of fabric for outer border.

BINDING

- Cut 5 strips 2¼" × width of fabric; sew together using diagonal seams.

Wouldn't this alternate red and green color combination make a great Christmas table topper?

Making the Blocks

All seams are ¼" unless otherwise specified.

This table topper has 12 half-square triangle (HST) blocks and 4 plain corner blocks. To create the star design, you will need 4 pieced/dark HSTs, 4 pieced/light HSTs, and 4 light/dark HSTs.

1. Sew together the 9 strips 1½" × 40" right sides together along the long edges to make a strip set; press. Subcut this into 4 pieced squares 8⅞" × 8⅞".

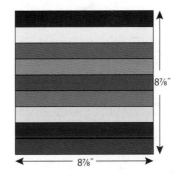

2. On the wrong side of 2 of the dark 8⅞" squares and 2 of the light 8⅞" squares, draw a diagonal line corner to corner. Set aside.

3. Place a pieced square in front of you, right side up, with the strips running *horizontally*. Place a dark square, right side down, on top of the pieced square, with the diagonal line starting in the top left corner and ending in the bottom right corner.

Note: Make sure all of your light and dark squares are placed on the pieced squares and sewn exactly like this!

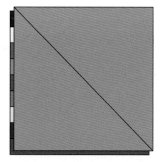

4. Sew a *scant ¼"* on each side of the drawn diagonal line. Cut on the drawn line and press toward the dark squares. Trim and square up to 8½" × 8½".

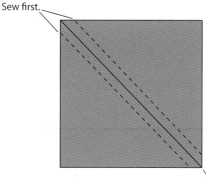

Sew first.

Cut last.

5. Repeat Steps 3 and 4 with another dark and pieced square to make a total of 4 pieced/dark HSTs.

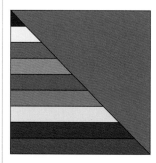

6. Repeat Steps 3–5 using 2 light squares and 2 pieced squares to make a total of 4 pieced/light HSTs.

7. Draw a diagonal line corner to corner on the wrong side of the 2 remaining light 8⅞" × 8⅞" squares. Place a light square on top of a dark square with right sides together, and sew a *scant ¼"* on each side of the drawn diagonal line. Cut apart on the drawn line and press toward the dark squares. Trim and square up to 8½" × 8½". Repeat with the last set of dark and light squares to make a total of 4 dark/light HSTs.

Assembling the Table Topper

1. Refer to the assembly diagram to lay out the blocks in 4 rows of 4, being careful to orient the darks and lights as shown.

2. Sew together each row and press the seams in alternate directions from row to row.

3. Sew together the rows and press.

Tip

To ensure nice crisp points that are not chopped off, when I got about 2″ from the intersection of two blocks while sewing the rows together, I lengthened my stitch to a basting stitch and sewed over the intersection and past it about 2″ and then decreased my stitch length back to regular size and kept on sewing until I got to another intersection. The method to my madness here is this: If there was a problem with the intersection or it didn't look good, I could easily pick it out and ease the seam where needed. If it looked good, then I just sewed over it with a regular stitch length and called it good!

---

4. This quilt has butted borders. Please refer to Quiltmaking Basics (page 57) to measure and sew the inner and outer borders.

Assembly diagram

Finishing

Refer to Quiltmaking Basics (pages 57–60) to layer, quilt, and bind your quilt.

Lil' Ditty Bag

Designed and made by Mary Cowan.

FINISHED BAG SIZE: 11″ × 15½″

I love this drawstring bag! It goes together so fast, and it's an awesome way to use up bigger fabric scraps. It's really useful for keeping small handwork projects like appliqué or knitting handy so you can just grab and go. There is an optional inside pocket for stowing small things. If you wanted to use vinyl-covered fabric for the lining, this would make a cute little lunch bag, too. Make them in different fabrics for all of your friends!

Materials

Fabric requirements are based on 40"-wide fabric.

- ⅓ yard of fabric for bag lower section and bottom

- ¼ yard of fabric for bag upper section

- ⅝ yard of fabric for lining and bottom and optional inside pocket

- ⅝ yard Decor-Bond Craft Iron-on Backing, 45" wide (see Resources, page 62)

- 1 yard cotton cording*

- Matching thread for topstitching upper section of bag

- Template plastic

* I found this in the curtain department at Joann Fabrics.

Cutting

Before you cut anything, choose which of the fabrics you want to use for the bag bottom and reserve a 9" × 9" square of that fabric. See the template pattern on page 56.

BAG LOWER SECTION

- Cut 1 rectangle 9" × 23¼".

BAG UPPER SECTION

- Cut 1 rectangle 7½" × 23¼".

LINING

- Cut 1 rectangle 16" × 23¼".

- Cut 1 rectangle 7" × 14" for the inside pocket (*optional*)

DECOR-BOND

- Cut 1 rectangle 17" × 24" for the bag body. Set aside the rest for the bag bottom.

> **Tip**
>
> *You will have enough to get the outside bag bottom piece from either the upper bag fabric or the lower bag fabric. You can decide if you want the bottom to match or to contrast. Ahhhh ... the choices you have!*

> **Tip**
>
> *When ironing the Decor-Bond to fabric, be sure to protect your ironing surface with Silicone Release Paper (see Resources, page 62).*

Making the Bag Body

All seams are ¼" unless otherwise specified.

1. Sew together the upper and lower sections, right sides together, along the long edges; press. This should now measure 16" × 23¼".

2. Following the manufacturer's instructions, iron the 17" × 24" piece of Decor-Bond to the *wrong side* of the bag. Trim off the excess Decor-Bond.

3. Fold the bag in half to find the center front. Using a very light pencil or water-soluble marker or chalk, mark 2 points at the center: one at 1¼" from the top and the other at 2¼" from the top. Draw a 1" vertical line for buttonhole placement between these 2 points.

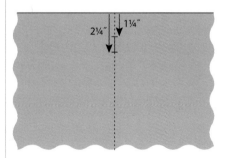

4. Make a 1" buttonhole using the buttonhole attachment on your machine, if you have one.

5. Fold the bag body right sides together in half and sew up the back seam. Press the seam to one side. You now have a "tube" with a buttonhole at the top center front.

6. For the bag bottom, trace the circle template (page 56) onto a piece of template plastic and cut it out. On the Decor-Bond, trace around the template twice. Rough cut outside the traced lines.

7. Iron 1 of the rough-cut Decor-Bond circles to the wrong side of your chosen bag bottom fabric, following the manufacturer's instructions. Cut out on the template line.

8. Pin the bag body to the bag bottom with right sides together and the bag body facing up. This is tricky, but if you go slowly, ease the fabric, and pin a lot, you should be fine. Sew them together with the bag bottom facing up beginning at the back seam. If you end up with more bag body than bottom, just make your seam allowance in the back of the bag body a little bit bigger—nobody will ever know!

Making the Bag Lining

1. Fold the pocket piece in half with right sides together. Sew around all sides, leaving a small opening for turning. Turn right side out and press. Eyeball where you want the pocket on the lining, pin, and sew it on around 3 sides. Make sure that the small opening for turning is on one of the 3 sides that is sewn down.

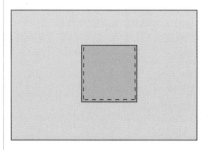

2. Sew up the back seam of the lining, leaving about 4" open in the middle for turning the whole bag right side out later. Press seam to one side.

3. For the bag bottom lining, iron the remaining Decor-Bond circle to the wrong side of your bag bottom lining fabric, following the manufacturer's instructions. Cut out on the template line.

4. Sew the bag bottom lining onto the bag body as described in Making the Bag Body (Step 8, at left).

Tip

Pay attention to which way will be "up" when sewing on the lining bottom—you don't want your pocket to be upside down! (Don't ask me how I figured that one out—let's just say there was some unpicking involved.)

Assembling the Bag

1. Turn the lining right side out and keep the bag body inside out. Put the lining inside the bag body and line up the back seams (nest these seams to avoid bulk). (The right sides should be facing each other.)

2. Pin around the top and sew together.

3. Carefully pull the bag through the opening in the lining seam, turning it right side out. Sew up the open seam in the lining and push the lining down into the bag body. Smooth everything out and make sure the buttonhole is in the center front.

4. To form the casing, place 2 tape guides on your sewing machine 1″ out from the needle and 2½″ out from the needle. Pin very well, or you will get puckers. Topstitch 1″ and 2½″ from top.

> ### Tip
> *In addition to pinning well, use a walking foot when topstitching the casing. It will help reduce puckers.*

5. Feed the cotton cording through the casing using a safety pin. Tie the ends together in a knot.

You are now done—I hope you enjoy your *Lil' Ditty* bag!

Bag bottom

Cut a total of 4:

• 2 from fabric
 (1 lining, 1 outside fabric)

• 2 from Decor-Bond

Lil' Ditty bag pattern

Quiltmaking Basics: How to Finish Your Quilt

General Guidelines

Seam Allowances

A ¼″ seam allowance is used for most projects. It's a good idea to do a test seam before you begin sewing to check that your ¼″ is accurate. Accuracy is the key to successful piecing.

Pressing

In general, press seams toward the darker fabric. Press lightly in an up-and-down motion. Avoid using a very hot iron or over-ironing, which can distort shapes and blocks. Be especially careful when pressing bias edges, as they stretch easily. Arrows are provided for pressing.

Borders

When border strips are cut on the crosswise grain, piece the strips together to achieve the needed lengths.

Butted Borders

In most cases the side borders are sewn on first. When you have finished the quilt top, measure it through the center vertically. This will be the length to cut the side borders. Place pins at the centers of all four sides of the quilt top, as well as in the center of each side border strip. Pin the side borders to the quilt top first, matching the center pins. Using a ¼″ seam allowance, sew the borders to the quilt top, and press toward the border.

Measure horizontally across the center of the quilt top, including the side borders. This will be the length to cut the top and bottom borders. Repeat the pinning, sewing, and pressing process outlined above.

Backing

Plan on making the backing a minimum of 8″ longer and wider than the quilt top. Piece, if necessary. Trim the selvages before you piece to the desired size.

Batting

The type of batting to use is a personal decision; consult your local quilt shop. Cut batting approximately 8″ longer and wider than your quilt top. Note that your batting choice will affect how much quilting is necessary. Check the manufacturer's instructions to see how far apart the quilting lines can be.

Layering

Spread the backing wrong side up and tape the edges down with masking tape. (If you are working on carpet you can use T-pins to secure the backing to the carpet.) Center the batting on top, smoothing out any folds. Place the quilt top right side up on top of the batting and backing, making sure it is centered.

Basting

Basting keeps the quilt "sandwich" layers from shifting while you are quilting.

If you plan to machine quilt, pin baste the quilt layers together with safety pins placed a minimum of 3"–4" apart. Begin basting in the center and move toward the edges, first in vertical, then horizontal, rows. Try not to pin directly on the intended quilting lines.

If you plan to hand quilt, baste the layers together with thread, using a long needle and light-colored thread. Knot one end of the thread. Using stitches approximately the length of the needle, begin in the center and move out toward the edges in vertical and horizontal rows approximately 4" apart. Add two diagonal rows of basting.

Quilting

Quilting, whether by hand or machine, enhances the pieced or appliquéd design of the quilt. You may choose to quilt in-the-ditch, echo the pieced or appliqué motifs, use patterns from quilting design books and stencils, or do your own free-motion quilting. Remember to check your batting manufacturer's recommendations for how close the quilting lines must be.

Binding

Trim excess batting and backing from the quilt, even with the edges of the quilt top.

Double-Fold Straight-Grain Binding

Piece the binding strips together with diagonal seams to make a continuous binding strip. Trim the seam allowance to ¼". Press the seams open.

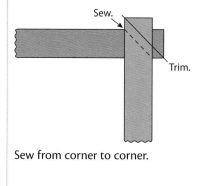

Sew from corner to corner.

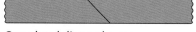

Completed diagonal seam

Press the entire strip in half lengthwise, with wrong sides together. With raw edges even, start sewing the binding to the front edge of the quilt in the middle of one side of the quilt. Leave the first few inches of the binding unattached.

Stop ¼" away from the first corner (see Step 1), and backstitch one stitch. Lift the presser foot and needle. Rotate the quilt a quarter-turn. Fold the binding at a right angle so it extends straight above the quilt and the fold forms a 45° angle in the corner (see Step 2). Then bring the binding strip down even with the edge of the quilt (see Step 3). Begin sewing at the folded edge. Repeat in the same manner at all corners.

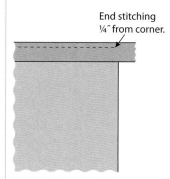

Step 1. Stitch to ¼" from corner.

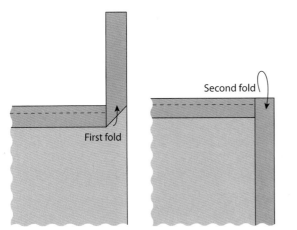

Step 2. First fold for miter   Step 3. Second fold alignment

Continue stitching until you are back near the beginning of the binding strip. See Finishing the Binding Ends for tips on finishing and hiding the raw edges of the ends of the binding.

Continuous Bias Binding

A continuous bias involves using a square sliced in half diagonally and then sewing the triangles together so that you continuously cut marked strips to make continuous bias binding. Cut the fabric for the bias binding so it is a square. For example, if yardage is ½ yard, cut an 18″ × 18″ square. Cut the square in half diagonally, creating 2 triangles.

Sew these triangles together as shown, using a ¼″ seam allowance. Press the seam open.

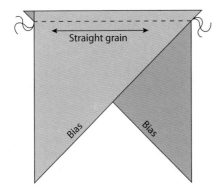

Sew triangles together.

Using a ruler, mark the parallelogram created by the 2 triangles with lines spaced the width you need to cut your binding. Cut about 5″ along the first line.

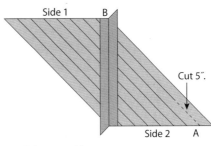

Mark lines and begin cut.

Join Side 1 and Side 2 to form a tube. The raw edge at line A will align with the raw edge at B. This will allow the first line to be offset by 1 strip width. Pin the raw edges right sides together, making sure that the lines match. Sew with a ¼″ seam allowance. Press the seam open. Cut along the drawn lines, creating a continuous strip.

Press the entire strip in half lengthwise with wrong sides together. Place binding on quilt as described in Double-Fold Straight-Grain Binding (page 58).

See Finishing the Binding Ends for tips on finishing and hiding the raw edges of the ends of the binding.

Finishing the Binding Ends

Method 1
After stitching around the quilt, fold under the beginning tail of the binding strip ¼″ so that the raw edge will be inside the binding after it is turned to the back of the quilt. Place the end tail of the binding strip over the beginning folded end. Continue to attach the binding, and stitch slightly beyond the starting stitches. Trim the excess binding. Fold the binding over the raw edges to the quilt back, and hand stitch, mitering the corners.

Method 2

See our blog entry at www.ctpubblog.com, search for "invisible seam," then scroll down to Quilting Tips: Completing a Binding with an Invisible Seam.

Fold the ending tail of the binding back on itself where it meets the beginning binding tail. From the fold, measure and mark the cut width of the binding strip. Cut the ending binding tail to this measurement. For example, if the binding is cut 2¼″ wide, measure 2¼″ from the fold on the ending tail of the binding, and cut the binding tail to this length.

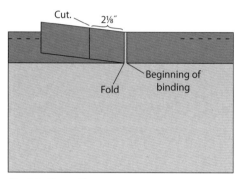

Cut binding tail.

Open both tails. Place one tail on top of the other tail at a right angle, with right sides together. Mark a diagonal line from corner to corner, and stitch on the line. Check that you've done it correctly and that the binding fits the quilt, and then trim the seam allowance to ¼″. Press open.

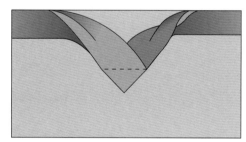

Stitch ends of binding diagonally.

Refold the binding and stitch this binding section in place on the quilt. Fold the binding over the raw edges to the quilt back, and hand stitch.

About the Author

Photo by Leslie Orme

Mary Stewart Cowan took up quilting in 1992 and began designing patterns about ten years later. She enjoys the entire quilting process, but her first love is fabric. She is passionate about color and loves changing the look of a quilt by simply using a different color scheme. She likes a wide range of different color schemes, from soft pastels to Civil War reproductions to the vibrant fabric designs of Kaffe Fassett. If you ever pass her booth at Quilt Market or Quilt Festival, you will see a lot of different types of fabric.

Mary's background in graphic design inspires her patterns. She earned a Bachelor of Fine Arts degree in graphic design from the Rochester Institute of Technology. She loves putting blocks together and discovering the secondary designs that occur when two blocks touch. She always has a pad of paper in her purse so she can sketch her latest thoughts. "I see things all around me that inspire my designs," she says. Mary lives with her husband and two kids in Utah—where she is spoiled by the many beautiful quilt shops nearby!

Resources

EZ QUILTING BY WRIGHTS
www.ezquilt.com

Tri-Recs Tools Tri Tool
(by Darlene Zimmerman and
Joy Hoffman)

No-Melt Mylar Template
Plastic

JO-ANN FABRICS
www.joann.com

Decor-Bond Craft Iron-on
Backing
(by Pellon)

Heat*n*Bond Lite
(by Therm O Web)

C&T PUBLISHING
www.ctpub.com

Silicone Release Paper

Quilter's Freezer Paper Sheets

the Quiltmaker's Club

More Patterns for Less

In this new series, we are gathering fabulous projects from established patternmakers into affordable books, all with the same high quality and accuracy you've come to expect from us. Now you get more patterns and more value!

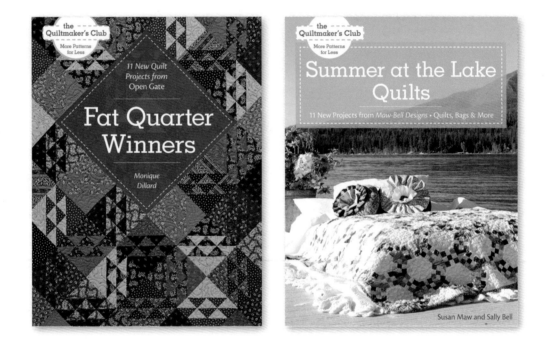

Available at your local retailer or **www.ctpub.com** *or* **800-284-1114 (USA)** ▪ **925-677-0377 (International)**